EMPIRES IN COLLISION

GEORGE E. VANDEMAN

Pacific Press Publishing Association
Boise, Idaho
Oshawa, Ontario, Canada

Unless otherwise indicated, Scripture references in this book
are from the New International Version.

Edited by Randy Maxwell
Designed by Tim Larson
Cover photo by Donald E. Carroll/Image Bank©
Type set in 10/12 Century Schoolbook

The author assumes full responsibility for the accuracy of all
facts and quotations cited in this book.

Copyright © 1988 by
Pacific Press Publishing Association
Printed in United States of America
All Rights Reserved

Library of Congress Catalog Number: 88-62692

ISBN 0-8163-0812-8

88 89 90 91 92 • 5 4 3 2 1

Contents

Before You Turn This Page . . .

For thirty-two years it has been my privilege to speak to the heart of this nation and overseas by way of television—an awesome responsibility, considering the nature of the message I feel compelled to share.

And of the twenty-five books coming from our presses, which have helped make the spoken messages permanent in the hearts of our hearers, this one—*Empires in Collision*—is to my mind the most significant and urgent.

Simply said, this book contains the unfolding drama of the great controversy between Christ and Satan that is moving with breakthtaking speed into its climactic moments.

To make these pages live via television, I have recently completed a 25,000-mile taping trip with my production staff to capture the evidence of this drama in living color. I hope that you, the reader, can relive the saga on television as well as through these printed pages.

And finally, I'm pleased to acknowledge the splendid assistance of Steven Mosley, an author in his own right, in the research and final preparation of this manuscript.

My hope and prayer is that the revelation within these pages will encourage you to make the Word of God your survival guide through the coming crisis.

—George E. Vandeman

Chapter 1
One World—Two Empires

The words echo out in different languages. But the faces are much the same. Anger, hatred, and violence flare out—in the name of religion. We preach love and understanding. We all denounce bloodshed. No one wants it.

Why, then, are so many believers caught up in it?

Isn't religion supposed to bring reconciliation? Why has so much blood been shed in the name of the Prince of Peace? And in the name of Allah? And in the name of Jehovah?

What's behind this unholy, never-ending conflict?

Down a certain road in 1947, hundreds of thousands of Moslems fled north to their new homeland, Pakistan, leaving ancestral lands, homes, possessions, jobs—everything behind. And on the same road they met countless other refugees fleeing south—Hindus leaving all they possessed for India.

The partition of India into two nations, one Moslem and one Hindu, produced an upheaval of epic proportions and unleashed hatred that had been simmering for centuries.

I was there that eventful year and remember vividly the refugees on those roads fleeing for their lives. Moslem majorities in the north set upon their Hindu neighbors with startling vengeance, slaughtering men, women, and children.

Hindus in the south attacked the Moslem minorities around them, killing old and young with abandon.

Perhaps the most frightening bloodshed occurred along railroad tracks, where trainloads of the uprooted were stopped and ambushed. There were days when not a single train got through without its burden of the dead and wounded.

Those who lived through this holocaust would never forget the sight of trains arriving at Lahore or Amritsar, doors opening, and blood pouring out on the platforms.

The carnage between Hindu and Moslem was so intense and widespread, so pitiless, that many veteran soldiers said, "It was far worse than anything we saw in World War II."

How can human beings slaughter the helpless? How can people kill children in their mothers' arms? Why does it seem the worst horrors are perpetrated in the name of religion? We wonder.

Perhaps we Christians may feel a bit superior about the so-called heathen killing one another. But tragedies like this are not restricted to the exotic Orient. We in the West also have our horror stories, our long tradition of bloodshed in the name of God.

It happened in Paris in the middle of the night. At 1:30 a.m., August 24, 1572, a bell began to ring in the cathedral tower of St. Germain l'Auxerrois. The tolling bell sent a signal throughout the city: death to the Huguenots.

France, at the time, was maneuvering for power between two enemy nations, Anglican England and Catholic Spain. The majority of Frenchmen were Catholics, and in the tense political situation, their fear and hatred of the Huguenots, the Protestant minority in their midst, had intensified.

Powerful Catholic nobles succeeded in persuading the French king to eliminate this troublesome minority. And tragically, many Frenchmen were willing to wield weapons against their neighbors of a different faith.

So on that terrible night, as the bell tolled, Christian men rushed out into the streets with swords and clubs. Huguenot men, women, and children were dragged from their homes and murdered.

The killing started near the Louvre, where the leader of the

Protestants was staying, proceeded to the Ville, then on to the university quarter; the streets ran with blood.

In the morning, the citizens of Paris were met with an incredible sight. The Seine River, which cuts a lovely green swath through this city of eternal spring, was littered with thousands of bodies. The Seine flowed red.

It was St. Bartholomew's Day. On this holy day honoring one of Christ's twelve disciples, men who professed to follow Christ massacred others who also called on His name. And the slaughter spread to several French provinces.

Tens of thousands of Huguenots were butchered in cold blood because their faith was judged impure.

What kind of madness drives people to do this? We wonder. It's hard to understand. Something terribly demonic happened on St. Bartholomew's Day, 1572. And it strikes uncomfortably close to home. It wasn't Hindus and Moslems slaughtering each other in far-off India. It was Christians passionately wielding the sword against fellow Christians.

Even more disturbing is the fact that the shouts of those who make enemies by their faith still ring out in our world, loud and commanding: Protestants and Catholics still battling it out in Northern Ireland. Christians against Moslems in Lebanon. Shiite Moslems persecuting Bahais in Iran. And on and on.

Killing for God. Why is the world convulsed with it? I'd like to suggest what might seem a disturbing answer. There are many political and social factors involved. But I think we can get behind the scenes and see a larger picture, larger forces at work in our world. To get this perspective we must go back in time to the very first conflict.

It happened in heaven, of all places. Lucifer, a brilliant archangel, became proud. Caught up in his high position, he began grumbling about God's getting all the glory. The Bible gives us a glimpse of this in Isaiah 14:13, 14: "You said in your heart, 'I will ascend to heaven; I will raise my throne above the stars of God; . . . I will ascend above the tops of the clouds; I will make myself like the Most High.' "

Instead of enjoying God's fellowship, Lucifer wanted to compete with Him.

He challenged God's right to rule. Lucifer the archangel turned into Satan the accuser. Finally he led a third of heaven's angels in open rebellion against God's government. The book of Revelation tells us: "There was war in heaven. . . . The great dragon was hurled down—that ancient serpent called the devil or Satan, who leads the whole world astray. He was hurled to the earth, and his angels with him" (Revelation 12:7-9).

War in heaven. Sounds almost impossible, doesn't it? But because God had created beings with free moral choice, the possibility existed that someone, sometime, could choose to oppose Him. Satan was that first someone.

Now God could have immediately vaporized this ungrateful traitor who'd spread lies about Him, questioning His fairness and good will. But that would have left the universe with questions, with mistrust.

So God let Satan promote his alternative plan on Planet Earth. He would have a chance to prove that God's law was not necessary and that people could be happy without His fellowship. The universe would have a chance to see which way really was best.

Well, as we all know, Adam and Eve listened to Satan's sales talk in the Garden of Eden. They fell for his insinuation that God was holding something back from them; they bought into his promise that they would be like gods and never die.

And so Satan got a foothold and began to work out his alternative principles. He began to build his kingdom of darkness, his alternate empire.

In the chapters of this book you will discover just how vast and penetrating this evil empire has become.

Now remember how his empire started—in a war against God. Satan has been at war ever since, and it is a religious war. Satan animates man's worst passions in battling against God's way. He is trying to set up an alternative religious system.

We usually look for God's enemies amid some atheistic, secular power. And it's true that Satan works through godless regimes. But remember, he is not interested just in opposing God; he wants to *replace* Him. Satan seeks to counterfeit genuine faith in God and genuine religious experience. He wants to rechannel our zeal, not snuff it out. He seeks to capture those on fire for God with other blazing passions. Satan attacks God through religion.

Remember that the next time you see the contorted face of some fanatic on the news, shouting death to the infidel, the next time you see the faithful slaughtering each other. Satan is involved in a *religious* war. His greatest triumphs come when he uses religious fervor to arouse our most intense hatreds and cruelest instincts.

Now God did not simply give up Planet Earth to Satan's evil empire. He planted the seeds of His own righteous kingdom ages ago in the mind of Abraham.

He nurtured into being a people who lifted up His true way in the midst of idolatry and corruption: "Thou shalt love the Lord thy God with all thy heart and soul and mind, and thy neighbor as thyself." For centuries the nation of Israel kept His law alive and continued the ceremonies that pointed toward a Saviour. Humanity always had a choice.

And God always had His witnesses to His truth. These prophetic witnesses climaxed in the coming of Jesus Christ. Jesus swept through Galilee and Judea, healing the sick, casting out demons, and proclaiming that the kingdom of God had arrived, in power, on the earth. Here was God's ultimate counterattack: the establishment of the true empire, based on the principles Christ embodied and taught.

Here was a charismatic Leader who aroused intense religious fervor—yet did not call for the blood of infidels. Instead, He shed His own blood on behalf of His unbelieving enemies. Instead of fighting sin with a sword, He took upon Himself its inevitable penalty.

Christ's empire was founded on the cross, on His life

sacrificed for our sins—and that empire was to spread throughout the world and challenge Satan's dominion. Matthew 28:18-20 records Christ's great call to build His empire in the world. "All authority in heaven and on earth has been given to me. Therefore go and make disciples of all nations, baptizing them . . . and teaching them to obey everything I have commanded you."

Now, as you look over the world, it may seem that the forces of darkness are overwhelming favorites. After two world wars and the genocide of Armenians, Jews, and Cambodians—all in this century—it may appear that hatred and violence, greed and lust have won. Hope, for many of us, is hard to come by. But, believe me, there is another empire at work on our planet.

God's conquests happen all the time, all around the world—wherever His Word takes hold of human hearts. God's victories are dramatic, but the drama takes place within. He builds up His empire from the inside out.

The way of love and reconciliation has had its victories, remarkable victories. Let me tell you about just one.

It happened in India, the same land where religious strife has taken such a heavy toll.

In 1867 a Norwegian missionary named Lars came to live among two-and-a-half million people called the Santal. They lived in a region to the north of Calcutta.

Lars demonstrated great ability as a linguist. He soon became so fluent in Santal that people came from miles around just to hear this foreigner speak their language so well. And so he began to talk about Christ's great kingdom to these people; He explained the good news of salvation.

Now Lars, like many missionaries, wondered how many years it would take before these people, so far removed from Christian influence, would show an interest in the gospel, how long it would take for them to open their hearts to this very different good news.

Well, to Lars's amazement, the Santal were immediately

electrified by what he was saying. After a while, one of their leaders exclaimed, "What this stranger is saying must mean that Thakur Jiu has not forgotten us after all this time!"

Lars caught his breath, astonished. Because he knew that *Thakur* was the Santal word for "genuine," and *Jiu* signified "god." The genuine God? Lars realized he was not introducing some new concept by talking about the one supreme God.

And so he asked, "How do you know about Thakur Jiu?"

The Santal replied, "Our forefathers knew Him long ago."

Lars then asked, "Since you know about Thakur Jiu, why don't you worship Him instead of the sun, or worse yet, demons?"

The Santal faces around the missionary grew wistful. "That is the bad news," they replied. And then a Santal sage stepped forward and said, "Let me tell you our story from the very beginning."

The sage proceeded to tell a history of how mankind had become alienated from the true God that, amazingly enough, paralleled the Bible story.

"In the present age," the sage said, "it is said by some that the sun god is Thakur. But the forefathers taught us that Thakur is distinct. He is not to be seen with fleshly eyes, but he sees all. He has created all things. He has set everything in its place, and he nourishes all, great and small."

Lars listened with growing excitement. Here a people had been prepared to receive the good news, just as the Jews were prepared by their sacrifices and ceremonies to receive Christ as the Messiah. The missionary discovered that generations of Santal children had grown up hearing their elders exclaim, "Oh, if only our forefathers hadn't made that grievous mistake we would still know Thakur Jiu [the genuine God] today! But as things stand, we've lost contact with Him."

Well, almost before Lars realized what was happening, he found himself with thousands of inquirers on his hands, begging to know how they could be reconciled to Thakur Jiu through Jesus Christ. They were thrilled by the thought that their sins could be forgiven, that the rift between themselves and the genuine God could be healed.

And healed it was. Soon Lars was reporting back to Europe as many as eighty Santal baptisms a day. Converts began to reflect Christ's character. And they bravely took the gospel still further among their own people.

The good news bore good fruit. In Lars's Santal mission alone, 85,000 believers were baptized, and many other missions were created to evangelize and train those who had been waiting so long for Thakur Jiu.

Satan has spread his empire far and wide. He deceives and seduces and bullies people into his evil empire. But God is at work on our planet too. He has planted seeds in people's hearts all over the world that wait to sprout and bloom. He seeks to win them to genuine faith through a loving witness.

One world—two kingdoms. Two empires competing for the allegiance of mankind. Friends, they are about to collide as they never have before. A confrontation is coming which will overshadow all previous conflicts. The book of Revelation paints a very vivid picture of this struggle that will climax earth's history—a life-and-death struggle over the hearts and minds of every inhabitant of this planet.

Battle lines are being drawn right now. The enemy is fine-tuning his greatest deceptions, his most seductive lies. It's not always easy to tell the two clashing empires apart. Sometimes they seem to overlap. Tragically, some who profess to proclaim Christ's kingdom really advance the alternative evil empire. The church itself can become corrupted, its voice distorted, its hands bloodied.

In the following chapters you will discover just how the empires will collide. You'll see where the battle fronts will be. And you will understand the truths that will stand at the center of the conflict.

Through God's Word we *can* see the overall picture, we *can* gain a definite sense of where we are going and what we'll be facing in the future.

And that's what we want to share in this book, *Empires in Collision.* Because when the two empires are seen clearly and their principles spotlighted, we'll be able to make the right choices—in the end. We'll be able to stand for the truths that are eternal. And we'll be able to find a hope in the one kingdom that lasts forever.

Chapter 2

The Steep Stairs to God

The devout on the banks of the Ganges at the end of a long pilgrimage, seeking to cleanse their sins away in its sacred waters. Believers in the Philippines flagellating themselves as they struggle on a pilgrimage toward perfection. Thousands of miles and thousands of years of cultural development separate these two groups, but, incredibly enough, they are both part of one vast empire.

To understand this, let's first travel to the city of Rome to a church called Santa Maria d'Aracoeli. Originally an early Christian basilica, it was rebuilt by the Benedictines in the thirteenth century. Its marble steps—there are 122 of them leading up to the church—tell an interesting story. In 1348, a terrible plague struck the area and took many lives. The survivors, of course, felt very grateful. And they decided to make an offering to God, so they constructed 122 marble steps leading up to His sanctuary.

It's a long way up to the church. I can't say exactly what the motives of the survivors were who had those beautiful marble steps built. I'm sure most were simply grateful, sincere believers. But they've left for us a striking picture of our human dilemma.

For many people, the way up to God seems long and steep. How do we climb the steps up to God's holy place? How do sinful human beings gain acceptance before a holy God? We all

17

want to survive the plague of sin, don't we? We all want God to save us. And many of us feel we must bring something to Him, an offering, some gift that will earn us acceptance.

How do sinful human beings get up to God? On that question hangs the central difference between the kingdom of Satan and the kingdom of Christ, the two empires which are headed for an apocalyptic showdown.

Satan's evil empire may manifest itself in violence, hatred, and lust. But at its root, it's a religious rival to the kingdom of Christ, a religious alternative.

If Christ offers us the promise of union with our heavenly Father, Satan must try to match that claim. He must construct a counterfeit way to God, a way that appears to make us like gods.

For a further perspective, we could travel on to one of India's many holy sites. In the temples of India, elaborate ceremonial offerings are made to various Hindu gods. By these special offerings, the devout hope to gain merit with their chosen deity.

Here ascetic holy men practice their harsher form of piety. By abasing the body, they hope to become totally identified with their god. Others hope to become one with the divine through lengthy meditation.

The waters of the Ganges River are considered sacred. The river is said to bring purity, wealth, and fertility to those who bathe in it. For Hindus, the most sacred spot in the world is where the Ganges merges with the Jumna River. Here millions gather during certain celebrations to immerse themselves in its purifying waters, hoping that their sins will be carried away. Many make long pilgrimages to die there, believing they will thus attain a higher status in their future lives.

Basic to Hinduism are the beliefs that one is earning bad or good karma in this life and that karma will follow him after death and cause him to be reincarnated as a lower or higher form of life. In Hindu morality tales, a foolish man is reborn as a monkey, a cunning one as a jackal, a greedy one as a crow.

Gaining merit, or good karma, can be attained in various ways—by righteous deeds, self-denial, Yoga, special knowledge, or devotion.

India is a sobering spectacle for anyone who takes the spiritual life seriously. Nowhere does one see a more earnest pursuit of the holy, in so many ways. India has been called "a land obsessed with God." In some ways it puts the materialistic West to shame.

And yet still, one gets the impression of people climbing steps, a steep series of steps that go on and on, with no end in sight. People slowly, over many lifetimes, working their way up to God.

Of course it's easy for us to dismiss the Hindu religion as the primitive pursuit of those who simply don't know better. But let's bring this problem of the long, steep steps a bit closer to home. Christians, too, have found a way to try to work their way up to God.

On many holy days in the Philippines you will see devout worshipers slowly trudging along roadsides, whipping themselves—they are the Flagellantes—agonizing on the path toward perfection. Some carry heavy burdens as they walk; some beat themselves; some crawl on hands and knees. All hope that their acts of devotion will win favor with the saint, and, through him or her, with God.

These people believe in Jesus. They believe that He died for their sins. But still the prevailing idea is that one must earn a right to that grace. In this world of penitence, saints and purgatory, the concept of earning merit weighs heavy on human souls. Again those haunting steps come to mind, those long, steep steps leading up to God.

Is this only a Catholic problem? We Protestants don't have our shrines to the Virgin Mary or prayers for those in purgatory. But I'm afraid we, too, have been haunted by those steep steps, in the form of legalism. For Protestants it has taken many forms.

The Puritans, for example, certainly trusted in the merits

of Christ alone. Salvation, they believed, came by faith. But that was sometimes obscured by their tendency to promote purity by a rigid set of rules. The terribleness of sin sometimes swallowed up the wonder of forgiveness.

Legalism still raises its ugly head today. We still get stuck on performance as a way to earn points with God. We accept Christ's free gift of salvation—and then try to pay Him back for it. It's as if we think the down payment on heaven is paid in full, but the monthly installments on the mortgage are real killers—that *we* have to pay.

Those long, steep steps can haunt us all. And friends, that is the alternative that Satan has constructed. It's his counterfeit gospel—working our way up to God. Righteousness by works. He has built up a vast empire based on that principle. All over the world people have bought into his system.

It is a prison within which millions of sincere people labor, on and on, never quite reaching the top of the stairs. Satan's empire is secure as long as he can keep people struggling on, focusing on their efforts, straining after merit, hoping against hope that just a few more steps will take them finally to God.

Christ's empire, though, is built on an entirely different principle. The man who rediscovered it for us in the modern world embarked on a pilgrimage of his own in 1510 to the holy city of Rome.

In that year two monks were sent to visit the Pope in order to settle a dispute that had arisen in their Augustinian order. One of the monks was named Martin Luther. He considered it a wonderful privilege to be able to visit the Eternal City. Here was a grand opportunity to claim the enormous spiritual benefits available in the city.

Luther set out to celebrate mass at sacred shrines, visit the catacombs and basilicas, venerate the bones of martyrs, pray at their shrines, and adore every holy relic.

But slowly this monk became disillusioned. It was a time of increasing corruption in the church under the Renaissance popes. The Italian priests he met seemed almost flippant about their duties. He was shocked by stories of immorality among the clergy.

And at this point the lone monk in a vast city of holy places began to doubt. He wondered whether a holy shrine or relic could actually convey merit.

And now we come to a series of steps that would change Christendom. Luther began climbing up "Pilate's stairs" where it was believed Christ had stood. Here on his hands and knees, the monk repeated the Lord's Prayer at every step, kissing each one—all in the hope of delivering a soul from purgatory—when suddenly, having arrived at the top, Martin Luther raised himself and exclaimed, "Who knows whether it is so?"

At that climactic moment, he dared to challenge Satan's alternative system of works. He had stopped the endless climb for a moment, the climb of Hindu, Buddhist, Moslem, Jew, and, yes, Christian too.

Luther's doubt was at first only a despairing thought: if these means of merit prescribed by the church could not really bestow grace, what hope was there?

But fortunately, Luther's spiritual crisis led him eventually to search into Scripture for answers. He dug deeper, began to study the book of Romans, and fell headlong into grace. Paul's exposition opened up for Luther the wonder and glory of Christ's great empire built on faith alone.

Luther had rediscovered the gospel. Specifically, he had uncovered the truth of justification by faith, which the apostle Paul so clearly laid out in his priceless epistle, that letter written, fittingly enough, to the people of Rome.

The apostle actually became well acquainted with the capital of the Roman Empire. He went there in A.D. 60 to appeal his case to Caesar as a Roman citizen. The Jewish leaders had accused him of sedition and wanted him put to death. Paul spent two years in the city under house arrest. It was there that he wrote his epistles to the Philippians, Colossians, and Ephesians.

It is believed that the apostle was finally granted a trial before Nero, acquitted, and set free.

But some time later, Paul was arrested again and brought back to Rome. This time he was chained in a cell, treated like a criminal. Many of his friends deserted him. Only Luke remained, faithful to the end, when the apostle was executed. But through it all, Paul maintained a confident faith and a deep assurance about his relationship with his Lord. He faced death triumphantly.

When we read his letter to the church at Rome we understand why. In Paul's day, Imperial Rome had placed most of the world under Roman law. From the plains of Central Europe to the Mediterranean shores of Northern Africa, countless tribes and peoples were subjected to the precepts of Caesar. In this epistle, Paul introduced the idea that everyone in the world is under a higher law, God's law. He declared that "the whole world [is] held accountable to God." And then he made this startling statement: "No one will be declared righteous in his sight by observing the law" (Romans 3:20).

Obedience to the law doesn't earn us acceptance with God? This sounded absurd to both Jews and Greeks. What other way could there possibly be? If we don't make progress up those steps by doing what God says, how *do* we get to the top?

And that was Paul's point. He wanted to turn people toward an entirely different hope. He was attacking Satan's empire at its root, firing an opening round at the devil's master plan of getting people to work their way toward heaven.

Paul explained that the law makes us ever more conscious of our sinfulness. We all fall far short of God's standards. And then he came to the heart of the gospel with this statement: "All . . . are justified freely by his [that is, God's] grace through the redemption that came by Christ Jesus" (Romans 3:23, 24).

Now let's look at this carefully. We are justified. That's a legal term. It refers to acquittal in a court of law. We are declared innocent; we gain right standing. Sinful human beings can be declared righteous by a holy God. How does this happen?

By grace, through Christ's redemption. Christ paid a ransom, by His blood on the cross. He laid down His life to pay the penalty we deserved. He paid our debt. He presented His perfect life as a perfect fulfillment of the requirements of the law. And so we can be redeemed, set free.

Now this is wonderful, glorious news for all of us trying to climb up that steep, endless flight of stairs. And Paul wanted to be crystal clear. He said that God justifies the man who has faith in Jesus. Faith in Jesus. That's it. That's the requirement. That makes justification possible. Not long pilgrimages. Not endless meditation. Not beating our bodies and praying before shrines. Not even the strictest adherence to Christian standards. None of that will justify a person. None of that will earn us acceptance with God.

Paul now zeroed in an artillery barrage on Satan's empire of works. He boldly proclaimed in Romans 3:28: "We maintain that a man is justified by faith *apart* from observing the law."

Heavy stuff. A direct challenge to Satan's alternative religious system. When people understand that God extends His full acceptance as a response to simple faith in Jesus, Satan's empire begins to crumble. Hindus caught in an endless round of ritual, stop and look up. Catholics bowed down under a burden of penance, stop. Protestants trying to pay God back in some way for His mercy, stop.

Yes, and Luther, who'd climbed up those sacred stairs in Rome, finally stopped and beheld the glorious good news for the first time. Paul's uncompromising theme became Luther's battle cry, "The just shall live by faith."

The rest is history. Luther proclaimed justification by faith; many in the church rediscovered the gospel. A reformation transformed Europe.

I think the people who built those 122 marble steps leading

up to their church did give us a useful symbol after all. The way up to God *is* steep; it *is* long. There *is* an immeasurable gulf between the holy God who is a consuming fire and human beings steeped in cruelty and vice.

But there is Someone who has come down from heaven and made the difficult journey up to God *for us*. There is One who has earned merit, obeyed the law, satisfied justice, *for us*—Jesus Christ.

God justifies the one who has faith in Christ Jesus. He takes him all the way up the stairs. That is the good news that has built up Christ's kingdom on this earth. That good news has set free countless people, all over the world, from the evil empire of works.

The two empires are heading for a showdown. Satan seeks in ever more ingenious ways to entrap people into his no-win system of works. Christ seeks to rescue and set free more and more people through the good news.

The gospel is the difference. It is the primary battleground between these two empires. Other issues arise, other controversies flare up, other battle lines are drawn, and we will be dealing with these in the next few chapters, but the fundamental conflict will always be the same: the gospel, the answer to that eternal question—how do we climb those stairs up to God?

The book of Revelation describes the two empires in conflict at the end of the world. In Revelation 14, we get a glimpse of God sending out His final warning to mankind through three angels. This is how the apostle John describes it: "Then I saw another angel flying in midair, and he had the eternal gospel to proclaim to those who live on the earth—to every nation, tribe, language and people" (Revelation 14:6).

How will God introduce His final appeal to mankind? By proclaiming the eternal gospel. That's the truth that needs to be defended. That is the object of Satan's attack. He has a vast assortment of tricks, counterfeit instruments of grace that will take our faith from the Jesus who justifies the ungodly.

Satan's self-help methods can sound very sensible. His techniques for attaining godhood can seem very noble. But they all end up depositing us on that endless staircase.

Have you placed your faith entirely in the righteousness of Christ? Does your hope rest entirely on His saving works and not your own?

The choice is yours. Two empires open up before us. The entrances to them may not seem that far apart at first. But they lead off into vastly different worlds. Make sure you go through that one narrow door that says, "God justifies the one who has faith in Jesus."

Chapter 3
War Over the Word

Paris, the city for lovers. The city of eternal spring. It's hard to imagine that, down its elegant boulevards, past its majestic cathedrals, and beside its graceful fountains, once thundered the call to revolution. It seems such a long way from those idyllic scenes to the reign of the guillotine.

Liberty. Equality. Fraternity. The French were the first to shout those revolutionary words over feudal Europe, interrupting a centuries-old chain of absolute monarchs. A famous Paris monument, La Republique, honors the men who struggled to bring about the continent's first democratic republic.

In a time when the church stood for the rich and powerful and the upper classes thought it a God-given right to dominate society, these men rose up to claim the rights of the common man.

The French Revolution introduced all these grand ideas. And yet it would be a long time before France became a truly democratic republic. The ideals of democracy succumbed to the Reign of Terror.

Maximilien Robespierre, foremost revolutionary leader, became, in effect, absolute dictator. And for a time, his principal tool of government became the guillotine.

Why? Why did such high ideals spawn such horrible bloodshed? I think one key reason is the revolution's intense attack on religious authority.

The people who stormed the Bastille, in the name of liberty, eventually came to impose their own atheistic religion on the people. The party in power, called the Jacobins, set up a new Revolutionary Calendar. They rejected the common calendar which dates years from the birth of Christ and set a new center point for time: September 22, 1792, the foundation of the Republic. This marked the beginning of what they believed was a new era in history. An era no longer under God.

The Jacobins actually declared Christianity illegal. Baptism and communion were prohibited. Copies of the Scriptures were collected and publicly burned. A municipal leader exclaimed, "We have expiated in a great fire all the fooleries which [these Bibles] have made the human race commit."

The promise of liberty, equality and fraternity turned into rule by the guillotine. God's law had been rejected, His authority discounted. And so, for a time, the darkest forces held full sway, unbounded by the Word.

Since then men have continued to seek freedom as an alternative to the authority of God's Word. And often they have ushered in other reigns of terror, even more tragic holocausts.

I believe God has an alternative to these failed attempts at liberty. While establishing His kingdom on the earth, Jesus told His disciples this: "If you abide in My word . . . you shall know the truth, and the truth shall make you free" (John 8:31, 32, NASB).

Jesus said freedom resulted, not from tearing down false authority, but from adhering to the right one: His Word, God's truth.

Christ's kingdom is built on the authority of God's Word. It is what keeps His empire of righteousness going. His eternal kingdom is based on His eternal Word. As Isaiah said, "The grass withers and the flowers fall, but the word of our God stands forever" (Isaiah 40:8).

In opposing Christ's kingdom, Satan always seeks to attack the authority of the Word. That is one of the cornerstones of his evil empire. Sometimes Satan tries a frontal assault, as he did through the leaders of the French Revolution. At other times he is more indirect. Sometimes the church itself can get in the way of the Word.

St. Peter's Basilica in Vatican City is the largest and most splendid temple-palace in all of Christendom. It is a masterpiece of architecture and art. Towering above the church's facade is the magnificent dome designed by Michelangelo.

Inside St. Peter's, visitors are awed by brilliant color and intricate craftsmanship as they walk down the soaring central nave leading to the gilded Bernini altar.

There's a very special sensation you get walking in the huge courtyard that is St. Peter's Square. The basilica rises toward the heavens in front, and a majestic colonnade, designed by the artist Bernini, encircles you. The columns, the statues, the sculpted walls, the lofty dome—all these dwarf the visitor. You become very small, humbled before these soaring works of art built to the glory of God.

Many people come here to renew their faith, and their faith *is* renewed amid the splendors of the church. The struggle to live a genuinely Christian life in a largely indifferent world can often be rather lonely. But here Christian themes find a heroic, triumphant echo.

I believe we can be thankful for those artists and artisans in the past who used their talents to make a statement of faith. But we must also be very careful. Because sometimes the church can become too majestic, too powerful for its own good.

Remember, we explained that Christ's empire is built on His Word, on the authority and power of His Word. Unfortunately sometimes the church has tried to usurp that authority and that power. It begins to see itself as the keeper of the Word, and then as the institution that places its stamp of approval on the Word.

The Word must be interpreted and applied. And so the church begins to interpret and apply authoritatively. Instead of leaving room for the Holy Spirit to convict individual hearts of truth through Scripture, the church defines truth once and for all. Tradition slowly takes on more authority than God's Word itself. And truth is confined within church dogmas.

But friends, God's truth marches on. He has wonderful truths for all of us to learn. It's a tragedy to stand still over some cherished church tradition. God wants us to progress, catch new light, see new truths unfold—*all* within the teaching of His Word.

Without this kind of growth, we fall backward. If we're not reaching out for more of God's light, the shadows are gathering around us. There are two competing empires in this world: the empire based on God's Word and the empire that undermines that authority.

Satan attacks the Word directly, through mockery and violence, and, more subtly, through religious tradition. But there is still another threat to the Word, this one even more subtle still, from a source few of us would expect.

The capital of India, New Delhi, is a city full of temples of almost incredible variety. It's not just that both Hindu and Moslem shrines have found holy ground there. Just in Hinduism itself, the number of gods and their respective temples boggles the mind. In Delhi's narrow streets you can find almost every imaginable representative of deity. And a confusing assortment of beliefs confront those attempting to understand Hinduism. After immersing oneself in the teachings of various sects, some conclude that one can believe anything and everything.

The reason Westerners have had a hard time understanding the religions of the East is that the underlying premises are so different. There is a very different idea of truth operating here.

In Hinduism, truths do not compete so much as run parallel to each other; there is not *one* great truth that must be discovered, but many truths. They all lead like the spokes in a wheel to the center—to motionless peace, that point where struggle and desire cease. Truth is something subjective, something you find within yourself.

In the last few years this way of thinking has invaded the Western world to a great extent. We talk quite readily now of "finding your own truth." People are more tolerant in a way, because all beliefs are considered more or less equal. We constantly hear appeals to look within for ultimate answers. People confidently assert that God is found in our innermost hearts.

The Bible, however, points us in a very different direction. It focuses on God and His eternal principles. God's moral expectations don't vary from day to day. He doesn't keep revising His law. God's truth is objective; it *does* compete with all other truths.

But many people today are losing their ability to understand that. For them truth is subjective—whatever you feel it is, whatever works for you. This, perhaps more than anything else today, is warring against the authority and power of God's Word. It is, I believe, a key element in Satan's evil empire. If he can get people cut loose from God's Word, they may drift almost anywhere. And people usually drift away from the call to the higher, moral life and toward their natural impulses.

Satan is carrying out a threefold attack on God's Word, through militant atheism, religious tradition, and the belief that *truth* simply lies within. His kingdom moves forward on three fronts. It's a vast empire, worldwide in extent. And friends, it's an empire of lawlessness. Without the strong pillar of God's Word and His law to cling to, we invariably plunge into lawlessness.

It's a flood that seems to be gaining ground everywhere. Look at any major city. Pornography abounds; crime is out of hand. We've fallen into our own Reign of Terror. Drug trafficking continues unabated—imprisoning the successful, maiming our young. Sexual perversion advertises itself as freedom of choice. Millions have the unborn killed routinely—as a means of birth-control. The public is scandalized by the misbehavior of "me-first" politicians and businessmen and, yes, religious leaders.

Lawlessness. That's when Satan's empire rears its ugly head. And this will be a critical issue during the climax of earth's history. The book of Revelation, in chapter 12, pictures a great conflict between the devil, called the dragon, and Christ's true church, symbolized by a pure woman. Verse 17 says: "Then the dragon was enraged at the woman and went off to make war against the rest of her offspring—those who obey God's commandments and hold to the testimony of Jesus."

What characterizes faithful believers at the end? They cling to God's commandments and Jesus' testimony. They haven't watered down God's law or made Jesus' teachings relative. They are not among the lawless of Satan's dark empire. They uphold the authority of God's Word.

To get our bearings again, in the empire of Christ, let's look back to the man honored by that magnificent basilica in Vatican City, the man whose bones rest under its soaring dome: Peter, apostle of Jesus Christ. What did he have to say about how Christ's church is made strong and what it is founded upon? I believe that his writings deal effectively with each of Satan's end-time attacks on the Word.

In opposition to militant unbelief, Peter raises up this mighty defense: "By God's word the heavens existed and the earth was formed out of water" (2 Peter 3:5).

Do you want to destroy the Scriptures? Then you had better destroy all of creation as well. Because the amazing variety of plant and animal life you see around you bears witness to God's creative Word. Graceful gazelles, towering oaks, and thundering waterfalls all testify to the power of His commands. He speaks and it comes to pass.

You can pile up Bibles and burn them, you can mock the Scriptures and outlaw them, but God's Word will always spring up again. It is a living thing. Listen to Peter: "You have been born again, not of perishable seed, but of imperishable, through the living and enduring word of God" (1 Peter 1:23).

The Word of God is the imperishable seed that gives us new birth. Christ often compared His kingdom to the growing seed. Here we see clearly what it's based on: the living, enduring Word of God.

Against Satan's frontal assault, Peter raises up the eternal Word that will stand fast when all else has faded away. Now we move to another front where the empires collide: the nature of truth, Eastern religions turning the focus within. Peter speaks to this issue too, in 2 Peter 1:3: "His divine power has granted to us everything pertaining to life and godliness, through the true knowledge of Him who called us" (NASB).

How do we gain "everything pertaining to life and godliness?" Through a true knowledge of Him, a true knowledge of Jesus Christ. Knowing Christ is not a matter of contemplating our own spiritual worth; it is not just something we feel within. It is knowing real facts about a real Saviour who lived in a real Palestine in the first century. Now let's read the next verse: "He has granted to us His precious and magnificent promises, in order that by them you might become partakers of the divine nature" (2 Peter 1:4, NASB).

Eastern religions tell us we may gaze within and find our oneness with God. Scripture tells us we can become like God by means of His promises. We can rely on clear, objective statements made by Him. We have promises to hold, when we stand on the Word.

God's promises always pull us higher; we grow into God's nature. We find salvation in the life and sacrificial death of Jesus. The false promises of subjective religion just pull us inward; we become more like ourselves, we go nowhere, but remain securely within that other empire.

Now let's look at the last threat to God's Word: religious tradition. On this point Peter was crystal clear. Listen to this beautiful description of how Christ's empire is built: "As you come to him, the living Stone . . . you also, like living stones, are being built into a spiritual house to be a holy priesthood, offering spiritual sacrifices acceptable to God through Jesus Christ" (1 Peter 2:4, 5).

In this chapter, Peter identifies the living Stone as the cornerstone, Jesus Christ. He is the foundation we build on; every one of us builds on that one foundation. We are each living stones built into a spiritual house.

Peter was a religious leader whose authority as an apostle was greatly respected in the early church. But he did not try to become a cornerstone. He told people to build their lives on Jesus Christ the living Stone. And he said that would make the church prosper.

In 1209, near the Italian town of Assisi, a pious youth named Francis was listening to a service in the Portiuncula Chapel. The priest read from Matthew 10 the instructions Christ had given His disciples before sending them out to preach and heal. "Freely you have received, freely give. Do not take along any gold or silver or copper in your belts; take no bag for the journey, or extra tunic, or sandals or a staff" (Matthew 10:8-10).

Suddenly this young man saw his calling, clear as day. The words of Christ struck Francis with remarkable power. Right there he gave away his shoes and threw away his staff and belt. He kept only one plain woolen garment, bound around his waist with a rope.

More important, Francis caught the spirit behind Christ's instructions. He caught the spirit of total giving. And Francis of Assisi was propelled into a life that astounded all Christendom. He led like-minded brothers all over Europe, preaching peace and virtue, ministering to the outcasts and the diseased, possessing nothing, loving everyone.

Francis lived in a time when most people couldn't read the Scriptures. He hadn't had much opportunity to study the Bible. But this small sliver of God's Word that Francis *did* hear, went to the bone. It became authority and power. "Freely you have received." Those words were an imperishable seed; they bore abundant fruit. They became a promise of partaking in the divine nature, in God's spirit of giving. They became a living Stone on which Francis built a whole new way of life.

What a ringing testimony this man bears to us today. We who have the Bible all around us, yet seem to take it so lightly. Do we honor the whole treasure of God's Word with the same intensity that Francis honored those three verses?

We can be built up into a beautiful temple, if we stand on God's imperishable Word, if we take its principles as our authority, its promises as our truth and hope.

That's what the empire of Christ is all about. Satan's empire leads us to lawlessness. It is spreading everywhere today, leading toward a terrible climax. Christ's empire honors God's eternal law.

Plan to be part of His kingdom. Honor His Word in your own life because it will unfold before you the good news of salvation in Jesus Christ. Don't get left out in the dark of lawlessness. Make a commitment to follow the light of Christ's Word—wherever it may lead.

Chapter 4
The Demon's Domain

It is a wonderful symbol, the towering figure of "Christ the Redeemer," built in 1931 by the churches of Rio de Janeiro. Christ stretches out his hands over this Brazilian metropolis, embracing humanity, calling all to Himself, and standing over us in authority. It speaks of the vast reach of Christ's kingdom, Christ's holy empire. But when we go down from this mountain, to the streets below, we are surprised at the kind of kingdom this statue presides over.

Rio de Janiero is laid back, colorful, expressive, full of life. The people here don't seem quite as caught up in the intense material pursuits that drive most people into narrow ruts. Many of the North American tourists who flock down to this emerald playground by the Atlantic think of it as a place to let go, a place to lose one's inhibitions.

What most visitors don't notice is the unique type of religion practiced here. Christianity and the occult mingle to an amazing extent. Many of the devout worship God and make appeals to spirits almost in the same breath. In many of Rio's street-side stores you can find demons and saints doing good business together.

You find renditions of the crucified Christ accompanied by a bearded Exu, or devil, with pitchfork. Next to the Virgin Mary, you find a statuette of raven-haired Pomba Gira, the prostitute she-demon. Beside the painting of a medieval saint, a two-headed, androgynous devil.

At spiritist centers, worshipers go into hysterical trances in front of altars set with images of Christ and the Virgin Mary. Spiritists often define their practices as "working through the saints."

There are three principal cults in Rio. Candomblé, the oldest, is a combination of magical beliefs which slaves carried over from Africa and the medieval Catholic faith of their Portuguese masters. Belief in the healing powers of the saints is mixed with devil worship. Candomblé centers around calling on the powers of spirit deities to perform white or black magic.

Another cult aims specifically at communicating with the spirits of the dead. It is Kardecism, named after a nineteenth-century French school teacher who wrote under the name Allen Kardec.

This European brand of spiritualism was imported from France in 1858 via Kardec's writings. The séances of Kardecism are very different in style from the African drumming and chanting of Candomblé. In Kardecist meetings the congregation keeps quiet, music by Schubert or Chopin plays softly in the background, mediums sit around a table dressed in white and wait until one is seized by a spirit and begins to speak with a spirit's voice.

But the major spiritualist sect by far is Umbanda. It mixes elements from Candomblé and Kardecism—the occult and spiritualism are joined. And this combination, interestingly enough, has the most adherents. In Umbanda, a pantheon of demons preside over drumming, singing, and dancing. And efforts are made to communicate with the spirits of the dead.

This is not simply something the poor and illiterate engage in. As one observer said, "Here in Rio everyone is taking part—generals, government ministers, lawyers, architects, police chiefs, pop stars, civil servants. Deep down, they all believe in magic and the supernatural."

Even those without religious convictions are won over by occult phenomenon. They are also won over because of the basic message presented: "There is no death." All of Rio's cults rest on one premise: people can make direct contact with spirits living in some other world, and those spirits can work for the welfare of men.

I believe this is one example of Satan's trying to counterfeit the claims of Christ. Satan wants to subvert the promises of the Redeemer who stretches out His arms above the city.

The kingdom of Christ offers a way out of death. And Satan, in order to build his rival empire, must try to offer an alternative hope. He has built an elaborate world of the occult to seduce people into his empire, offering what appears to be a way beyond the grave.

Satan is up against God's promise of eternal life. And that's why he desperately tries to fabricate an alternative hope, some way to ventriloquize a voice from the other side, some way to make death seem like life. He tries to focus our attention on spirits, or on some invisible soul cut loose from the body which he can manipulate.

Satan's alternative is not just confined to the exotic ceremonies of a South American metropolis. Like the other elements of Satan's empire, the occult has a very wide reach. It penetrates even through the sophistication of a city like Paris.

Many famous people are buried in that city's Père Lachaise Cemetery. The remains of the great painter Delacroix and the writers Marcel Proust, Victor Hugo, and Honoré de Balzac lie here. The great composer Chopin is buried here with a little soil he brought from his native Poland. Perhaps the most famous lovers in history, Abélard and Héloïse, have at last found union in this cemetery, buried side by side. Oscar Wilde rests here also, after a lifetime of turmoil.

These artistic geniuses have their admirers who come periodically down these cobbled paths with flowers. But, strangely enough, the greatest number of pilgrims visit the tomb of a man few of us remember.

The grave is that of Allan Kardec. Yes, the same man who inspired the cult of Kardecism in Rio. He is considered the father of modern spiritualism. In his most important work,

The Book of Spirits, he described supernatural phenomenon associated with séances, talked about voices from the other world, and discussed the nature of life after death. The book caught on in Europe and spawned countless séances and occult gatherings.

And the popularity of spiritualism persists. Periodically you will find thousands of flowers placed at this grave and a group of the faithful standing around, praying. One by one they step around to touch the left shoulder of his bust, their eyes closed.

Spiritualism still holds out that seductive promise: there is no death.

Walking among the tombs of Perè Lachaise, one gets the feeling they are all attempts to hope, in one way or another, ways to deal with that always unmanageable opponent, death. We try to make it something heroic, something noble, or something mysteriously beautiful perhaps.

And the world of the occult, the possibility of reaching out and touching someone—beyond the grave, proves to have a powerful appeal. We still fall for that old, old promise, "You shall not surely die."

Satan's empire stretches from Rio to Paris—and far beyond. It is an empire that has begun to encircle both East and West and unite them around a common occult vocabulary.

For centuries Hindus in India have clung to their own kind of hope for life beyond the grave—reincarnation. The Hindu faithful hope to attain merit that will help them achieve a higher state when they are reincarnated. This hope is based on something called the transmigration of souls. Eternal life is not something tied to God alone, they believe; it is tied to human souls. Does that ring a bell? Souls are immortal. And so when the body dies, the soul migrates to another body and is reincarnated. If one has lived a virtuous life, one can hope to come back in a higher caste or higher economic position. Reincarnation is the key to transcending the grave for the Hindu.

It's interesting to note that here, too, in this world of transmigrating souls, the occult thrives. In the Hindu pantheon, the distinction between gods who must be worshiped and demons who must be appeased is often hard to make. The Hindu cosmos is crowded with myriads of deities.

There is no simple sleep for the dead, and no single God in the heavens.

Now, reincarnation used to be one of those quaint beliefs you studied about in books on the Far East. No more. It is now a real alternative in the West too. The trendy now throw reincarnation costume parties: Come As You Were. Celebrities like Shirley MacLaine glamorize the theory. And the New Age movement enshrines it as clear and present dogma.

Nothing makes clearer the connection between spiritualism and the occult than the recent "channeling" phenomenon. "Channelers" claim to become possessed by the spirits of various departed wise men who convey messages from a cosmic realm. This channeling phenomenon has an almost exact parallel in the spiritist cults of Rio, where a medium goes into a trance and provides a spirit-being with temporary bodily existence.

The remarkable thing is that all these spirit-beings speak a very similar message: you are your own god, there is no right or wrong, just individual reality. Channeling as a whole seems to repeat a very old lie, told in the Garden of Eden: "You will be like God."

Satan's occult empire is serious. It is entrenched, and it has deeply infiltrated all religions. It is one of the battle lines drawn between the kingdoms of Christ and Satan. Their empires clash over the state of the dead and the hope of the living.

What does happen to a person at death? That, I believe, is the critical issue. Are there "departed spirits" who can communicate with us?

Jesus Himself has something to say on this subject. When news reached Him that His beloved friend Lazarus had died, Jesus told His disciples this, in John 11:11: "Our friend Lazarus has fallen asleep."

Our Lord saw death as a kind of sleep. Conscious existence ceases. The apostle Paul echoed this view. In writing to the Thessalonian church he described deceased believers as those who "have fallen asleep in [Christ]" (1 Thessalonians 4:14).

There is no place in the New Testament for transmigrating souls. No place for wandering spirits. No place for spiritualism. The dead are simply asleep. Period.

Often, in religious circles, we hear the phrase "man's immortal soul." But did you know that those words are never once used in the Bible? The same can be said for "immortal spirit." The Bible knows of a spirit of wisdom, a spirit of meekness. It is acquainted with unclean spirits, fervent spirits, and renewed spirits. But it is a complete stranger to any eternal human spirit.

Scripture does wax eloquent about the God who is alone immortal; it can't say enough about the everlasting covenant, the everlasting kingdom, the everlasting gospel. Scripture celebrates God's eternal power and eternal purposes; it boasts of a Word which abides forever.

But isn't it remarkable that none of those words are ever applied to the human soul! Not once.

The Bible's picture of our state at death cuts the ground from under Satan's occult empire. It states unequivocally: there can be no souls wandering about, no human spirits communicating with us.

Christ's solution stands in clear contrast to Satan's occult deceptions. Scripture does not view death as an underworld to be explored, but simply as sleep. And the only hope for an awakening is the resurrection of Jesus Christ.

Catch the contrast between the two empires in this verse: "Just as sin reigned in death, so also grace might reign through righteousness to bring eternal life through Jesus Christ our Lord" (Romans 5:21).

Now in Satan's kingdom sin reigns, sin dominates, and it does so "in death." Sin brings on moral and spiritual decay. Those in Satan's empire are dying, even if they appear to be hyperactive in evildoing. Sin invariably points people in a fatal direction.

Spiritualism makes a lot of promises about seeing beyond the grave and transcending death, but all the séances and occult ceremonies are really just about forms of death. They concentrate on vague disembodied states, voices from the dark, beings in some kind of limbo. There's no real human life there.

Something very different dominates in Christ's kingdom. Grace reigns; it reigns through righteousness, and it brings on eternal life. God's grace renews human life; it produces righteous lives, and those lives are headed toward eternal life. That's the focus of Christ's kingdom; it's headed toward eternal life, not disembodied limbo. And Scripture is very clear about the source of this eternal life. It is Jesus Christ.

All our hopes about a righteous quality of life that goes on forever must be tied firmly to Christ. The apostle John wanted to make sure we understood that. He wrote, in 1 John 5:11, 12: "God has given us eternal life, and this life is in his Son. He who has the Son has life; he who does not have the Son of God does not have life".

That's clear enough, isn't it? Eternal life is in Jesus. We don't get it anywhere else. We don't stumble across it in some séance. We don't run into it through a spirit mumbling in the dark. We don't find it within us through some occult experience.

No, it's only in one place—Jesus Christ. He is our hope. The Christ who died for our sins. The Christ who broke through the jaws of death, the One who resurrected and promises us a future resurrection at His coming. Paul makes that hope clear in 1 Corinthians 15:52, 53: "The trumpet will sound, the dead will be raised imperishable, and we will be changed. For the perishable must clothe itself with the imperishable, and the mortal with immortality."

When do mortal believers gain immortality? When the trumpet sounds, at Christ's second coming. Not before.

It happened in Scotland during World War II. A young woman received the dreaded notice that her husband was missing in action. At first she clung to the hope that perhaps he'd be found, that maybe, just maybe, there'd been a mistake. But months passed; no further word came, and finally this woman realized her husband wouldn't be coming back.

Then several friends, who had contact with a spiritualist medium, urged her to attend a séance and try to make contact with her deceased husband. The thought of being able to see and talk with the one she loved and needed so desperately had an irresistible appeal.

The young woman attended the séance. Contact was made; she recognized her husband's voice! During subsequent séances they talked over many things only the two could have known about.

And then one day this woman answered a knock on her door—and almost fainted to find her husband standing there—in the flesh, alive and well. There *had* been a mistake; he hadn't even been seriously wounded, much less killed.

Well, you can imagine the joy of that reunion. But imagine the wife's perplexity also. Who had she been talking to all this time? Lying spirits had taken advantage of her loneliness. This woman gradually became bitter and disillusioned with all religion.

Friends, there is only one hope for breaking through the grave, only one way to eternal life. There is only One who has conquered death for us: Jesus Christ who, after His crucifixion, resurrected and "appeared to many." He is the one and only source of eternal life.

Please don't get caught up in the hype and glory of Satan's miracles; please don't mistake forms of death for eternal life. The battle lines are drawn. Where is your hope? When you reach out and touch someone beyond the grave, make sure it is Jesus Christ and not some demon masquerading as a loved one. Only Christ can awaken us from the sleep of death. Make sure your faith is securely in Him as Saviour and Lord of eternal life.

Chapter 5
Back to the Garden

Versailles. Palace of Louis the Fourteenth, the Sun King. Here, Louis wanted a paradise, a place of exquisite beauty cut off from the problems of the world. And he got it. At Versailles, France's handsome, creative monarch produced a dazzling array of immaculate gardens and classically designed palaces. In such a paradise that delighted the senses, no one heard the approaching thunder of revolution.

No expense was spared to make the gardens of Versailles the most splendid in the world. Such a quantity and variety of flowers filled these gardens that guests were at times overwhelmed by the sight and smell. Sometimes they would pass through banks of exotic blossoms on their way into supper and then, as they returned to the gardens after the meal, find, to their amazement, that the beds and borders were now filled with masses of entirely different flowers.

Louis loved fountains. He had a total of 1,400 of them built on the palace grounds. And he wanted them constantly in play. This was impossible from an engineering point of view at that time; there just wasn't enough water pressure. So when His Majesty took strolls around the gardens, his servants had to frantically manipulate the taps so the right fountain came on as soon as the king came within sight of it and was turned off, to conserve the water supply, as soon as he passed it by.

Life at Versailles established an ideal—of sorts. The object of the games was pleasure—of the most extravagant and expensive kind. Operas and plays were sometimes commissioned and performed—just for the entertainment of guests.

A duchess observed that gambling was enthusiastically pursued. "The players behave like madmen," she declared, "screaming, striking the table, uttering blasphemous oaths."

And there was always a feast going. Louis loved to eat. A lady at the court declared that if she ate half as much as Louis she would be dead within a week.

Louis also consorted with a succession of mistresses. There was always some kind of sexual maneuvering going on at court. And although Louis detested it, homosexuality was rife among the courtiers at Versailles. One observer concluded that these social climbers had become bored with the easy charms of the women at the palace.

Life at Versailles seemed safely insulated within its well-financed pleasures.

But in the narrow streets of Paris, thirty miles from Versailles, there were no gardens or parties or elaborate costumes, just an endless struggle for daily bread. Lives walled in by poverty proceeded from desperation to despair to smoldering anger. Republican sentiments aroused the masses, and the people began to feel a revolution rumbling in their empty bellies.

It was a rumbling Louis the Fourteenth could not understand. Those closest to the king had concluded it was no use speaking to him about the miserable conditions under which most of his subjects lived; it merely made him cross.

Louis's successors also did little to reach beyond their paradise at Versailles. And so the smoldering anger turned into shouts of rage.

On October 5, 1789, the women of Paris, having formed their own regiments, marched on Versailles, armed and angry. In pouring rain, the mob swarmed around the gates, shouting threats. The fishwives and market women had had enough. "No more talking!" they yelled. "Bread! Bread! Meat at six sous the pound!"

The paradise at Versailles had come to an end. The revolution had come in earnest. The palace was ransacked; the royal family became refugees.

The golden age of Versailles passed away. But something of its spirit still remained. Even after the revolution, that promise of a material paradise persisted. In Europe the struggle to acquire creature comforts slowly began to replace the comforts of religion. A break with spiritual values was forming that would soon create a more secular world.

And then another kind of revolution arrived, the Industrial Revolution. For a time that material paradise seemed within reach. We were confident the machine could save us and usher in a new age.

Alexandre Gustave Eiffel, an engineer specializing in viaducts and pylons, decided that a tall tower would be just the thing to set off the Paris World Exhibition of 1889.

Here was a way to demonstrate what man could accomplish with his new industrial muscle. Here was a symbol of technological progress, a gravity-defying structure gracefully throwing its iron latticework 1,056 feet into the sky. It lifted up to the heavens a celebration of architectural and engineering skill.

In factories around Europe, machines were doing more in much less time than human laborers could ever hope to do. The world's leaders were looking forward to endless financial expansion via the Industrial Revolution.

The end of the nineteenth century was an age of optimism. Man was on a material ascent. From the peak of his technological progress he looked out on the world as master. Progress was the watchword of the day. People saw before them a limitless horizon.

And increasingly they did not find God on their horizon. Higher Criticism and Darwin's theory of evolution had cast doubt on God's Word. It seemed more reasonable to place faith in man and progress than in spiritual truths.

But then suddenly that optimistic age came crashing to a halt in a worldwide reign of terror—World War I. The machines that were supposed to save mankind could be used equally as well to destroy him. Tanks and artillery multiplied the carnage of the battlefield.

And the factory system in our cities produced its own kind of grinding poverty. The worker was locked into long hours of drudgery in an unhealthful environment, and he usually went home to a tenement crowded into the slums.

The poor remained. That material paradise always lay somewhere ahead, just over the horizon beckoning them on, enabling them to toil just one more day.

And so we've landed in a deeply secular age, founded on a belief that we can solve our problems without God. Driving the age forward is always the vision of a material paradise.

Today that old problem, the gap between the haves and the have-nots, has not gone away. By some accounts it has even been magnified—in spite of all our industrial resources.

I believe it's time we looked at an alternative. We've been pursuing the material paradise for so long that sometimes we forget there *is* something else to aim at on the horizon. The alternative is the kingdom of Christ. It stands in stark contrast to most of our preoccupations today.

In Christ's kingdom, success is measured by such things as meekness and mercy. The poor in spirit are respected, not shoved aside. It's those who seek God from a pure heart, not those who seek status symbols, who are considered most fortunate. And those who pursue righteousness and peace are blessed, not those in pursuit of a penthouse apartment.

Christ has built an empire on this earth based on those principles. And soon it will come into violent collision with another empire in hot pursuit of a material paradise, the empire of Satan himself.

Sometimes the devil attacks with banners blazing through demonic activity. Sometimes he makes a frontal assault by means of some persecuting, atheistic regime. But often he is content to seduce us into a pleasant slumber, surrounded by material comforts, insulated from God. He is quite happy to remain in the background as long as we remain in his empire of self-satisfied materialism.

The battle lines are being drawn right now between the empire of Satan and the empire of Christ. The book of Revelation describes that coming conflict. And it suggests that we can fix our aim on the right paradise by going back to our roots.

In Revelation 14, three angels are pictured flying over the earth, giving man his last message before the conflict erupts. This is what the first angel declares in a loud voice: "Fear God and give him glory, because the hour of his judgment has come. Worship him who made the heavens, the earth, the sea and the springs of water" (Revelation 14:7).

Here we are reminded to worship God as Creator, the maker of our material world. Our secular age has forgotten this important fact. We must trace our origin to a spiritual being; our roots are in Him. We do not go back simply to an accidental mingling of chemical material.

The second angel in Revelation 14 announces that Babylon has fallen. In ancient times Babylon was a very rich, indulgent city that often tried to dominate Jerusalem. In the Hebrew mind it suggested a materialistic and immoral way of life. And so Babylon came to symbolize the realm of Satan with all its seductive allure.

Well, the second angel was announcing that the empire of materialism is doomed. It is going to run into a dead end; its promise of paradise is an illusion.

Then the third angel speaks in verse 9. He delivers a very strong warning about worshiping the beast and his image. The beast was a symbol of Satan's representative on earth, the head of his vast alternative empire. And I believe the material paradise is part of that counterfeit system.

Now, in very forceful terms the third angel warns us about the fate awaiting those who give their allegiance to the beast.

He says: "If anyone worships the beast and his image . . . he, too, will drink of the wine of God's fury" (Revelation 14:9, 10).

Notice that here we see the counterpoint to the first angel's message. We are *not* to worship the beast; we *are* to worship the Creator. These two stand in opposition. The one calls us into Satan's empire, into his seductive vision of a material paradise. The other one calls us to give God glory, to worship Him as Creator. We need to get back past the secular age and find our spiritual roots.

Now, let me tell you about one way we can do this. It's something that many Christians have overlooked. The fourth commandment that God delivered to His people from Mount Sinai actually called them back to their origins, to their spiritual roots. It said this: "Remember the Sabbath day by keeping it holy. Six days you shall labor and do all your work, but the seventh day is a Sabbath to the Lord your God. . . . For in six days the Lord made the heavens and the earth, the sea, and all that is in them, but he rested on the seventh day. Therefore the Lord blessed the Sabbath day and made it holy" (Exodus 20:8-11).

The fourth commandment asks us to remember, remember the One who made the heavens and the earth. It is a weekly reminder of the day on which God finished His creation. This is a wonderful thing to have in our secular age—a tie in time back to our origins.

You see, we can look to the sun for our yearly cycle. And we can look to the moon for our monthly cycle. But there is no natural phenomenon to explain our weekly cycle. It is suspended alone in time, pointing back to the seven literal days of creation, back to the seventh day when God rested from His works and made something holy.

The Sabbath declares to a secular age rooted in materialism: Stop! Our roots go back to something else. We are tied to a Creator. We are not just material specks in a mechanical universe. We are spiritual beings with the ability to worship God Almighty.

There's another way in which the Sabbath functions as God's alternative to Satan's materialistic empire. It asks us to stop working. It ordains a break in that endless struggle for daily bread. Listen to this clear declaration in Hebrews 4:9, 10: "There remains, then, a Sabbath-rest for the people of God; for anyone who enters God's rest also rests from his own work, just as God did from his."

Do God's people still need a Sabbath rest? Yes. Now more than ever. The Sabbath gives us a chance to look up out of our rut. It gives us time to reach out toward that Creator who is still able to supply the needs of His creatures. The Sabbath reminds us we are all children of a God who cares. We are so busy trying to ensure material security we don't have time to look up to the Source of eternal security. But He *does* supply the needs of those who trust in Him.

Knowing the Creator, and taking time to worship Him, does make a difference.

The Sabbath is a wonderful answer for those caught up in the false promises of the material paradise. It can be our oasis in a spiritually barren world which glorifies material success. It can be our fertile garden where spiritual values blossom and bear good fruit.

It's tragic that all that beauty at the Palace of Versailles surrounded such corruption. King Louis did build something very worthwhile there; it's a masterpiece, it's inspiring—on the outside. These gardens have given enjoyment to thousands. But inside the walls, human nature indulged itself to death.

I believe that God calls us back to a beautiful garden. Back to the original garden, the original paradise which He created perfect, the paradise which the Sabbath memorializes. God spared no expense; He worked to make it the most beautiful in the world.

And there He wanted to have fellowship with us. That's what Christ's empire calls us back to, back to the garden. Back to our spiritual roots with our Creator.

Please don't let anything muffle that call. Don't let materialism dull your spiritual senses. Don't become deaf to the Spirit. Because you won't be able to hear the far-off rumblings of revolution coming closer. Insulated in comforts, you may fall asleep. And it won't be just an angry mob that interrupts your slumber. It will be God coming to the earth to make it new, coming to reckon once and for all with the beast and his evil empire.

Make sure you don't fall for Satan's counterfeit vision. Make sure you remember the Creator of heaven and earth, and worship Him alone. Take the wonderful gift of Sabbath rest. Take time to remember. Take time to worship. Take time now, before the clash of empires makes it too late.

Chapter 6

The Lamb That Roars

Rome. City of fountains and basilicas, statues and shrines. Classical works of beauty dominate the landscape. Here, history gathers to speak of passion and conquest, faith and sacrifice. And here we find the most graphic demonstration of two empires in collision.

Not much remains of the Forum—the heart of ancient Roman life—where the imperial government carried on its work. But once its stately columns welcomed worshipers into the Temple of Antoninus and Faustina.

Through the imperial chambers there passed Tiberius, Caligula, Nero, Domitian, terrestrial gods who governed, and sometimes squandered, the world. Now we see only ruins; then, one saw all around Roman power glorified, enshrined in marble.

Only a few columns remain of the Temple of Castor and Pollux, the twins whom legend has made the founders of the city. The temple was built in 484 B.C., after the victory of Rome's armies over the Tarquinians. Most of ancient Rome's monuments commemorated some military conquest.

And on the Palatine (next to the Forum) was the emperor's residence. Here the Caesars resided as gods. In Rome, religion served the needs of the state. In fact, church and state were almost identical. Roman emperors presumed to have divine authority for whatever they proposed.

In Rome today we can also see preserved one attempt of an emperor to deify himself—for posterity. Here Augustus, Rome's first emperor, built his mausoleum and the *Ara Pacis Augustae*, Altar of Augustan Peace. It was a peace based on conquest. The monument was built after Roman victories in Spain and Gaul had subjugated virtually all of Rome's challengers. The structure was designed actually as a representation in sculpture of the deeds of *Divi Augusti* "the divine Augustus."

Augustus, his family, and the consuls and officials of the imperial court are carved on the monument. These personages follow one after another in an imperial procession, solemn and heroic in their majesty. It is the self-portrait of conquerors, men who ruled the world.

Above all, Rome celebrated conquest. And their conquests included a small province called Judea. The Arch of Titus was erected by Domitian in honor of his brother Titus who had captured and destroyed Jerusalem in A.D. 70.

Carved reliefs inside the arch celebrate the victor leading away his captives and taking the city's spoils. There is one especially poignant scene: soldiers carrying aloft the seven-branched candlestick from the temple in Jerusalem. God's holy place had been raided and His people crushed.

Rome celebrated the religion of power. Its largest temple, the Temple of Venus and Rome, was built by another conqueror: Hadrian. Everywhere in the ancient city one could see temples commemorating military victories and the worship of gods who embodied the right of might.

It was this that made the Christians see in Imperial Rome a foreshadowing of the antichrist. In the book of Revelation, the apostle John makes many thinly disguised allusions to Rome. He saw it as a great beast doing the work of Satan, the dragon, in persecuting believers.

John was saying something important about Satan's empire and what it is based on. Satan seeks to conquer, by any means available. He creates a religion of power. He makes people believe in a god who forces his will on human beings.

Standing just beyond Hadrian's Temple of Venus and Rome one can see the place where the empire of Christ began. It is a most unlikely place for the beginning of a worldwide empire—the Colosseum. That is where the early Christian martyrs shed their blood in the name of Jesus Christ. They refused to pay homage to Caesar in Hadrian's Temple; they would not bow down to the emperor as to a god. They stood against a religion which used the state to enforce its dogma.

The empire of Christ began on the floor of the Colosseum, in silent testimonies before 45,000 Roman citizens yelling for blood. Today, we see only the underground cells where prisoners and wild beasts were kept, awaiting their fate. Back then, the floor of this amphitheater turned crimson with the blood of those who proclaimed their allegiance to Christ alone.

Thousands of believers were burned alive, crucified, or killed by wild beasts. Their testimony rang out loud and clear: allegiance to Jesus is more important than life itself. Their suffering was a silent protest against the religion of conquest, the religion of state power.

The bodies of the Christians were taken out through a small gate, the *Porta Libitinaria*, named after Libitina, the Roman goddess of death, and carried quickly away for burial in an unmarked grave—pathetic corpses seemingly insignificant compared to this great colossus of Roman might.

But the martyrs' testimony proved stronger than the sword of Rome. Their blood watered the seeds of faith in many other hearts. They became conquerors. The apostle John explains their triumph over Satan and his evil empire in this way: "They overcame him by the blood of the Lamb and by the word of their testimony; they did not love their lives so much as to shrink from death" (Revelation 12:11).

Christ's empire is based on sacrifice. It is built on a God who was willing to make the ultimate sacrifice. Jesus, God's Son, dying on the cross, seemed foolishness to the Romans. They mocked believers with cartoons of people worshiping a crucified donkey. But Christ's empire grew strong in spite of this, based on God's humiliation on Golgotha.

The Romans knew only one way to deal with opposition and rebellion—the sword. Their gods got their way by battling adversaries. Roman gods were conquerors. But the God of the Bible chose a very different way to deal with opposition. The cross was God's solution to human sin and rebellion.

He could easily destroy His adversaries. He could easily silence those who defy Him. God could have eliminated Satan when He first proposed an alternative to God's government. Instead He gave human beings freedom to choose. He would not force His way on us. He allows us to examine the alternatives, Satan's empire and Christ's empire, and make our decision.

God does not stretch out an imperial hand to force us to obey; He stretches out His arms on the cross, demonstrating His infinite love. God Himself chose to solve man's sin problem by taking on Himself our burden of guilt and paying its penalty. God draws people through love.

Sacrificial love. That's how God works. That's how His kingdom operates.

So here the two empires collided, conquering power versus sacrificial love. And sacrificial love eventually won out. Christianity flourished in the Roman Empire. The Christian church moved from the catacombs to cathedrals. Pagan gods gave way to Christian heroes.

But slowly, in this victory of the church, something happened. The eloquent testimony made by those willing to give all for their faith changed to a different kind of statement.

Another imposing monument in Rome is the Arch of Constantine, built in honor of Rome's first Christian emperor. It is called, significantly enough, the Triumphal Arch of Constantine. And it was erected to commemorate a military conquest, Constantine's victory over Maxentius at the Milvian Bridge.

The arch is decorated with sculptures and reliefs taken from the monuments of earlier emperors, Trajan, Hadrian and Marcus Aurelius. On a Christian monument, there are gathered those imperial faces in majestic procession, those rulers of the world, confident in their power.

Now that the church had overcome the world, through the blood of its martyrs, it tragically proceeded to copy the world. The arch reminds us of all the other arches and monuments commemorating Imperial Rome's conquests. It rises up in the same spirit. The church became powerful; the church became identified with the state.

Slowly pagan customs and practices crept back into Christian worship. And eventually the church that had worshiped fervently in the catacombs became the Holy Roman Empire.

Faith became something to be enforced, rather than proclaimed. Heretics must be burned rather than persuaded. Tragically, the heavy tread of Roman might echoed within the halls of the church itself.

Is this just a problem of the church in the Middle Ages? No, I believe it is a problem that will play a significant role in the earth's final conflict. It is one of the battle lines forming now between the empire of Christ and the empire of Satan.

John the Revelator saw it coming. Chapter 13 of his book of prophecy pictures a beast arising out of the sea to wage war against God's people. This is the final conflict. The beast is so powerful that it seems impossible to oppose its advance. Listen to this symbolic creature described: "The beast I saw resembled a leopard, but had feet like those of a bear and a mouth like that of a lion" (Revelation 13:2).

This beast is, in part, a combination of leopard, bear, and lion. You may recall that in the Bible's other apocalyptic prophecy, the book of Daniel, these beasts were used to describe the kingdoms of Babylon, Medo-Persia, and Greece, kingdoms that preceded Rome. So this final beast must symbolize Rome itself, the power that inherited the wealth and dominion of those previous world powers.

Only it was far more powerful, pictured as a seven-headed monster full of horns. For the early Christians, Imperial Rome did indeed play the part of the beast, a persecuting antichrist that did Satan's work. Verse 4 tells us that the dragon, that is, Satan, gave his authority to the beast.

But the book of Revelation, of course, is not just history; it very clearly points toward the last days, earth's final conflict. Its prophecies are given primarily to outline events which precede Christ's second coming.

So we must view this beast also as a power in the future, the final antichrist through which Satan makes his last stand. And Imperial Rome with its religion of power and conquest is the model on which it is built. John describes the end-time beast as an arrogant force that blasphemes God. This calls to mind the emperors who set themselves up as deities; their self-worship was a blasphemy against the holy God of heaven.

So we must look for a power that sets itself up in the place of God, a charismatic figure who calls for our worship. This will be the head of the enemy's vast empire in the end. He attempts to make his authority replace the authority of God. And he will rule by conquest.

John tells us, in Revelation 13:8: "All inhabitants of the earth will worship the beast—all whose names have not been written in the book of life."

Here Satan's vast empire becomes starkly visible. The beast draws the allegiance of everyone—except those whose faith is still firmly in Christ. It echoes those fateful days when the whole world seemed to obediently pay their worshipful dues to Rome's emperor—only Jesus' followers made a stand, a stand that often took them to the Colosseum.

Now later in Revelation 13, we come to a very interesting, and, for many, confusing second part of this prophecy. Let's read verses 11 and 12: "Then I saw another beast, coming out of the earth. He had two horns like a lamb, but he spoke like a dragon. He exercised all the authority of the first beast on his behalf, and made the earth and its inhabitants worship the first beast."

Here we see that the antichrist finds a great ally, some power that helps push the world toward the worship of the beast. Now, in the time of John, the cult of emperor worship fulfilled this role quite well. The second beast was the state religion that forced all Roman citizens to worship the emperor, the beast who persecuted believers.

But now let's think about the end times. How will this second beast function then? How will it aid the antichrist? Well, perhaps we have a clue in what happened in early church history. Remember that the church began through the testimony of martyrs on the floor of the Colosseum. Sacrificial love was the message. The early believers, one could say, were like lambs led away to the slaughter. Now the second beast is pictured with two horns like a lamb. It starts out like the gentle lamb, with its association with sacrifice.

But then it speaks like a dragon; the lamb begins to roar. It's an incongruous picture, isn't it? But that's exactly what happened to the early church. Remember the Triumphal Arch of Constantine? The church became powerful; it conquered. It began to enforce the faith. And finally it did speak with the voice of a dragon, a roar; it became itself a persecuting power just as Imperial Rome had been.

I believe this serves as a picture of things to come. We know that a persecuting, blasphemous power is coming in the end times. But how will it win over so many people all over the world? How can religious people possibly be made to worship Satan's representative? Because of the lamb that speaks like a dragon.

The church itself can fall into the power trap and lure us into Satan's kingdom. It can become a new cult of emperor worship, turning our faith toward some charismatic, powerful leader, instead of keeping it on Jesus alone. It can seek to enforce righteousness. It can seek to conquer through secular power instead of through its testimony of faith.

Can this really happen, people wonder, in modern times? The Inquisition carried on its gruesome work centuries ago. It's hard for us to imagine anything like that happening now.

Well, as it turns out, the Church of Rome is not the only one with a weakness for power. Good Protestant voices are being raised right now in the United States which, I believe, come close to that frightful roar of the beast.

Even in this land of democracy, lifting up its lamp for the huddled masses yearning to breathe free, even in this land which can appear so like a benevolent lamb, one can hear the rumblings of intolerance, the harsh voices of state religion.

Christians are having a hard time changing people. We feel threatened by the seductive, secular age. It seems so difficult for the gospel to really have an impact on society. We're losing our moral values. And so now many want to change laws. We say, maybe state-sponsored prayers in public schools will save us—maybe if all elected leaders were Bible-believing Christians—maybe if we could just set up the right standards.

Could the search for a political solution to spiritual problems be gaining a dangerous momentum? Some openly seek to restore a Christian theocracy in the United States and to begin enforcing all the social laws of the Old Testament. Could it be we aren't recognizing the implications of our sincere religious efforts?

Now it's our right and duty as Christian citizens to seek to affect the laws of the land. But I'm afraid for many it's gone beyond that. Our view of what Christian victory and triumph is has changed. The religion of power has slipped in; the possibility of political conquest beckons. We're tired of bearing witness to an indifferent world, people say; we want our voices to be heard. We're ready—to roar.

All of us must beware of the lamb that roars. Because there are only two empires out there. The empire built on sacrificial love and the one built on power and conquest. These are the choices that will confront us very soon.

As for me, I want to stand with those who testified so eloquently in the Colosseum. The beast roared all around them, demanding their blood. But the sacrificial love of Christ kept them strong.

We must be strong when confronted by the seductive

religion of power. We have to choose to win others by love and love alone. I hope you, too, will stand on that sacred ground, in the fellowship of those willing to give all, not take all, for the Lamb of God. There is no greater monument in this world. No marble temple can equal the eloquence of those lives given as sacrifices.

Let's join them. Now and at the end.

Chapter 7
My Children, My Blood

Greece, that cradle of democracy, has had its share of bloody struggles down through the years. One of its most wrenching conflicts occurred in the 1940s, when a civil war tore apart the nation already suffering through the bloodshed of World War II. It was a conflict which provides us with a telling glimpse of that greater clash of empires.

Two resistance groups claimed the hearts and minds of the Greek people, who had suffered much under German occupation. Communist guerrillas battled right-wing guerrillas for control of the villages scattered through mountainous Greece. Each group was determined to govern the country at the end of the war.

The Communist forces, called the Liberation Army, claimed to champion the cause of the poor against tyranny and injustice. They won many supporters.

They promised a new order based on justice and equality. They claimed to lead a people's struggle against poverty and humiliation.

The Communist guerrillas did succeed in ridding their areas of the bands of thieves that roamed the mountains, and they imposed a very strict code of justice on the villages they controlled.

But slowly that code of justice turned into a code of vengeance. At first only criminals and traitors were executed. But then the guerrillas began to shoot anyone who publicly disagreed with them. Whatever guerrilla leader happened to preside over a village could decide who lived and who died.

One of the tragic victims of this violent period was a woman named Eleni. Her son, Nicholas Gage, managed to piece together her story, years after he had escaped to the United States.

Eleni saw that the guerrillas in Lia, her tiny village, were forcing teenagers to join them in their fight. And there was talk that the Communists were going to send the younger children off to Albania for "reeducation." So this young mother determined to save her children.

Eleni planned an elaborate escape. Unfortunately, a villager betrayed her. Eleni managed to get her children out to safety, but she had to remain behind.

When the local guerrilla leader, a man named Katis, found out that Eleni had helped her family escape, he was furious. The man interrogated Eleni and had her tortured.

Then he gathered the residents of Lia together for a "people's trial." Katis read a long statement charging that Eleni was a known fascist and had stubbornly refused to send her children to the "people's democracies." He also accused Eleni of undermining the efforts of the guerrillas by organizing escapes from the village.

When neighbors stood up to defend Eleni, Katis promptly cut them off. He and two other judges retired for a few moments and then returned. Katis announced that the evidence against Eleni was overwhelming, and she was sentenced to death.

A few days later Eleni and several other condemned villagers were taken up into the hills to the execution grounds. Eleni stumbled along on legs black and swollen from torture. She looked thin and pale, near death.

But as one villager recalled, she mustered enough strength, just before the rifle shots rang out, to utter a terrible, piercing cry: "My children!"

Eleni was just one of the many victims of people like Katis, determined to force their version of justice on the world—by whatever means necessary.

It's a very tragic and very old story. Down through history, most of the suffering man inflicts on his fellow man comes from a desire to see justice done, our justice. And again and again, the code of justice turns into a code of vengeance.

I'm afraid that is the way we've looked at God too. We expect Him to dispense justice, of course. Religions all over the world include a picture of a final judgment. The ancient Egyptians, in their Book of the Dead, described in detail what happened to a soul coming before the judgment seat of Osiris, god of the afterlife.

Unfortunately, we look at God's justice through our own emotions. And an uncompromisingly just God can seem like a God of vengeance. A God who comes in judgment can seem vindictive.

This is a picture of our heavenly Father that Satan has gone to great lengths to reinforce. Nothing suits his purposes better than to have us fear a vengeful deity. Nothing furthers his vast empire on this earth more than the picture of an ill-tempered God who must be continually appeased.

So many religions are based on placating an angry god. Satan has bound up countless multitudes in a vicious cycle of fear and appeasement. An endless assortment of gifts are offered up to the moody sovereign on high. Some people are driven to the point of offering human sacrifices. Israel's Philistine neighbors even offered up their own children.

At first glance, the Hebrews themselves seem to fall into the same category. Didn't they offer up gifts to Jehovah? Didn't they lay blood sacrifices on an altar to atone for their sins?

Yes, they did. The book of Leviticus gives detailed explanations of required sacrifices. *But*, there was an important distinction in the offerings made by the Hebrews: everything pointed forward to a sacrifice *God* would make. Everything pointed forward to Christ's great sacrifice on the cross.

That's the crucial difference between the atonement in the Bible and other attempts at appeasement. In Scripture, God's sacrifice is at the center. In the alternative, man's sacrificing is at the center. Here is where two empires diverge. Here is where the kingdom of Christ and the kingdom of Satan divide. It involves the nature of God Himself. Is He a God who is moved to sacrifice Himself? Or is He only a God who demands human sacrifices?

The story of Cain and Abel makes this difference clear. A lot of us have wondered why Abel's sacrifice was accepted and Cain's wasn't. They both, after all, brought the fruit of their labors and offered them up to God. Abel, the shepherd, brought lamb portions, and Cain, the farmer, brought fruits and vegetables.

But, if we read carefully the account in Genesis 4, we notice that Cain was making an alternative offering God had not asked for. When Cain reacted angrily to the rejection of his offering, God told him, "If you do what is right, will you not be accepted?" (Genesis 4:7).

God seems to be saying, "I've told you the sacrifice that is right. That's all you need to do to be accepted." Cain seems to have stubbornly offered an alternative.

The offering God had in mind related to that garment of sheepskin that He used to cover Adam and Eve after they sinned. It related to the One who would come and crush the serpent's head. The lamb offering symbolized Christ.

What was Abel lifting up to God? A lamb, a symbol of Christ the Saviour, a symbol of the sacrifice God Himself would make. And what did Cain lift up? Fruits and vegetables, valuables intended to win God's favor, gifts to appease a moody deity.

You see the difference. One offering on the altar focused on the sacrifice God would make. The other centered on the sacrifice man was making. One reveals a God who is motivated by self-giving love. The other points at an endlessly demanding tyrant.

Now in the New Testament, the book of Hebrews shows us how these sacrifices, and the other services in the Jewish temple, relate to the judgment, to God's justice. The author of Hebrews explains how all the ceremonially shed blood of animals finds its fulfillment, its meaning, in the shed blood of Christ, the real sacrifice for sin. And he also points out that Jesus Himself is the ultimate high priest, the culmination of all the priests ministering in the temple who went before Him. Hebrews 8:1, 2 tells us: "We do have such a high priest, who sat down at the right hand of the throne of the Majesty in heaven, and who serves in the sanctuary, the true tabernacle set upon by the Lord, not by man."

Jesus Christ is serving as our High Priest right now, ministering in a heavenly sanctuary. And what do we find in that "true sanctuary"? God's throne of majesty. This is the seat of justice that Satan has endeavored to make so fearful. He wants us to think of the God who judges individuals from His great white throne as vindictive and endlessly demanding. But notice this wonderful fact: that throne of justice is *in* the sanctuary, the place where sacrifice is accepted, the place where God's blood shed on our behalf is accepted.

You see, Jesus Christ is there at the right hand of the throne. Jesus the high priest is our Advocate with the Father. Listen to how He is described in Hebrews 4:15, 16: "We do not have a high priest who is unable to sympathize with our weaknesses, but we have one who has been tempted in every way, just as we are—yet was without sin. Let us then approach the throne of grace with confidence."

Friends, we won't stand alone in the judgment. We have a sympathetic advocate there. And He presents His own sacrificial death as the basis of our pardon. He presents His own sinless life as the basis of our acceptance. God satisfied His own demand for justice. All who believe in Christ are accepted by the Father *in* the beloved Son. And so the fearful throne of judgment becomes a throne of grace. We approach it with confidence, because Jesus our High Priest has sacrificed Himself for us. That's the kind of God who is coming to judge the world, One who has sacrificed Himself for us. That makes all the difference—between Christ's kingdom and Satan's counterfeit.

We can see this reflected in the story of Nicholas Gage, the son of that heroic mother, Eleni, who saved her children at the cost of her own life. Nicholas grew up remembering the mother he'd been separated from at the age of nine, and he determined to find out all he could about her execution. Over the years he flew to Greece several times and visited the town of Lia and talked to villagers there about their memories of the civil war. Slowly he began to piece together the story of how his mother died. And through this he discovered the identity of her murderer, Katis.

Nicholas traced the man to the town of Konitsa. He decided to go there and find him. All the others directly involved in his mother's mock trial and execution were now dead. Only Katis remained, the man behind it all.

As Nicholas drove a rented car toward Konitsa, he thought of his mother's final cry—"My children." He had agonized for some time about how to respond to those heart-wrenching words. Had Eleni met death with acceptance, willing to defy a human command to honor a higher law of the heart? Or was she crying out for vengeance?

Nicholas arrived at the home of Katis and was invited in by his wife. After a few words of introduction, Nicholas said, "There was a trial of civilians in Lia in which you took part."

"No, no," Katis replied, "I tried no civilians."

"There were 300 villagers present," Nicholas answered. "They remember you."

Katis became very nervous and continued to deny everything. Nicholas pressed his accusations, his outrage mounting before this hard, unrepentant man. He clutched a revolver in his pocket, ready at the least provocation to kill the one who had heartlessly tortured and murdered his mother.

But then Nicholas realized that if he killed Katis, he would also have to kill his wife, too, and also a grown daughter who was in the house. Otherwise he'd never get away.

Nicholas abruptly left and slammed the door behind him. There was no doubt in his mind now that Katis deserved to die. Justice demanded it. He had seen arrogance and the cold indifference of a killer in the man's eyes. Nicholas vowed to confront the man again, this time when he was alone.

Four months later, Nicholas found his man vacationing in a port on the Ionian Sea. He waited outside his apartment until he saw Katis's family leave and head toward the beach.

Then Nicholas forced the lock open on the front door and slipped inside. There in front of him lay the executioner, fast asleep. This was it. The moment he'd been waiting for. Nicholas wouldn't even have to use his gun. He could just smother the old man. The family would return and find that Katis had died in his sleep. No one would suspect anything.

Nicholas stepped forward, but then the memory of Eleni overtook him—his mother's gentle touch, her loving words. Nicholas had learned much more about her since he'd begun investigating her tragic death.

One witness had told him that on the day before her execution, Eleni did not speak of the pain of her torture, but only of her longing to embrace her children one last time. That's what she lived for; there was little room for hatred in her life.

The film based on Nicholas's book brings this out in a memorable scene. Eleni has just realized that she will have to stay behind in Lia in order for her children to escape. Bidding them farewell, she clutches Nicholas, her only son, and whispers to him with great emotion, "My heart, my blood!" As Nicholas stared at his mother's executioner, he realized that her final cry was not a curse on her killers. It was an invocation of what she had died for, a declaration of love: "My children!"

And at that moment, Nicholas wanted Eleni's love to live on in him, and in his children. He didn't want the cycle of injustice and vengeance to continue. Nicholas was able to look through the killer toward his victim and see the beauty of his mother's sacrifice. He turned around and walked out of the house, closing the door softly behind him.

Friends, that's what the judgment is all about. It's not an opportunity for vengeance. It's an opportunity for God's beautiful sacrifice to shine forth.

God *is* a judge; He is passionately concerned with justice. But He is also our High Priest, our Intercessor. He presents His perfect life and shed blood as our substitute. He satisfies His own demand for justice—at great cost to Himself. That is the foundation of His righteous empire.

What a picture we have of God—if we see the judgment in a sanctuary setting.

We have a heavenly Father who cries out, "My Children!" That's what He lives for. There's no room for hatred in His heart. He is identified with all who believe in Him, as their Priest. He has given His life for each of us. Love compelled Him to make the ultimate sacrifice.

We are guilty. There's nothing we can do to cover our shameful acts. We deserve to die. But God looks through all that and sees the sacrifice. Mercy and justice come together in that great act of love.

God wants us to escape from the clutches of sin, from a world gone mad with violence. And He is willing to go to any lengths to save us. When you look up at God Almighty and think of the judgment that will surely come on this cruel world, remember who the Judge really is. Remember how much He longs to save us. He longs to clutch us close and whisper, "My heart, my blood."

We have been purchased by the shed blood of God Himself. We are His cherished children!

Chapter 8
Who Owns the Future?

Napoleon Bonaparte has left us a magnificent symbol of his great empire—the Arch of Triumph. He dreamed of uniting all of Europe under his rule—and almost succeeded. For fifteen years he dominated the continent, until that fateful day when his army encountered Wellington at Waterloo.

How did Napoleon manage to draw a whole nation after him into wars of conquest? A nation that had just been through the wrenching chaos of revolution?

Napoleon had charisma. He built up a personal grandeur and glory that compelled millions throughout Europe to admire him. He was a man of keen intelligence and driving will who exercised an almost magical charm over those he met. And, most important, he inspired the French to dream big dreams. Napoleon's vision of a great French Empire that would dominate future ages compelled men to give their lives for him.

But, in a sense, Napoleon's empire ended up rather meekly at the Invalides Hotel. It was, and is, a barracks for old soldiers. It housed some of Napoleon's veterans, broken men missing arms or legs, men slowly dying of their injuries.

After Napoleon's defeat, France shrunk back to manageable boundaries. Europe returned to its previous rivalries and alliances. And the old soldiers whiled away their lonely hours at the Invalides Hotel talking over the great campaigns.

A glorious future, a vast empire that will endure forever, heaven on earth: such are the dreams that move nations into conflict. And Arches of Triumph are built. But over and over, broken human lives are all that's left in the wake of empire. And the stone monuments come to have a hollow echo.

This zealous pursuit of empire is one of the greatest tragedies men have had to endure over the years. And I believe it is a vital part of Satan's strategy in earth's end times. He wants more than anything else for people to transfer their hope of heaven to something here on earth. He wants to restrict their longings and dreams to something he can manipulate. And so Satan moves people to follow a charismatic leader into some great campaign; lives are caught up in an epic struggle for power—and then used up. Their strength and hopes are sapped, and they are left broken shells, sacrificed to the empty dream.

The kingdom that Christ has set up in this world stands in opposition to Satan's kind of empire building. Christ has made many promises, but one thing He has *not* promised is heaven *now* on earth. On the contrary, he assures believers that they may undergo hardship because of their faith. He pictures the spiritual life as one of struggle. Christ does not offer us an empire with observable boundaries.

We are urged instead to build a kingdom with its capital in heaven. We are asked to place our hope entirely on an empire that will take physical form only at the end of earth's history.

And yet the veterans of Christ's campaigns seem to have so much now. What a contrast they are to the veterans of those earthly empire builders. Christ's soldiers testify to a full life in His service; they inspire the next generation to give their all in spreading the good news of the kingdom. These veterans show us not broken bodies and wasted years, but healthy minds and full hearts.

We are told that in Christ's empire, to give up our lives is to find them. That's the paradox those caught up in Satan's empire can't understand. They're always running after the promise of heaven *now*.

Napoleon lies beneath an impressive dome, enshrined, admired, honored—and very still, his driving ambition finally quenched by the sleep of death.

The Invalides buildings laid out in their majestic beauty, in his honor, seem to still echo that hope of the eternal empire on earth.

Jesus Christ left us no monuments. What He did leave was a very significant absence: His tomb is empty. Christ didn't remain dead. Neither Roman soldiers nor Jewish leaders were ever able to produce the body they had so carefully secured in its tomb. No one found any remains.

Having completed His campaign on this earth, Christ was resurrected, and He ascended up to heaven.

The apostle Peter believed that Christ's ascension is the key to our hope as human beings. He wrote in 1 Peter 1:21: "Through him [that is, Christ] you believe in God, who raised him from the dead and glorified him, and so your faith and hope are in God."

Why are we able to have faith and hope in a God who is far off in heaven? Because Christ has been here! He was raised from the dead. And while human eyes were fixed on Him in wonder, He ascended up into glory. That's why we can look up with confidence. Someone we know is up there preparing to come again, preparing to make His empire a physical reality on this earth.

Listen to what two angels told the disciples gazing up into the sky after their ascended Lord: "This same Jesus, who has been taken from you into heaven, will come back in the same way you have seen him go into heaven" (Acts 1:11).

The coming of Christ is going to be every bit as real as His first visit on our planet. The promise of Scripture is crystal clear.

Satan doesn't want us looking up. He wants, at all costs, to keep us looking for a heaven on earth *now*. If only he can keep us following after some charismatic figure with big promises, he can prevent us from discovering the true hope of Christ's eternal kingdom.

Tragically, the church itself hasn't always helped us look up. Early Christian believers fixed their gaze firmly in the heavens, hoping in the return of Christ. But during the Middle Ages that hope slipped away. The church on earth busied itself consolidating its powerful position. As the Scriptures were largely replaced by church tradition, the prophecies of a second coming were lost sight of.

By the eighteenth century, another important element began to narrow the church's vision: rationalism, the belief in man's reason, as opposed to God's revelation, as the starting point for understanding all things. Many became skeptical of anything supernatural. Scholars attempted to divest the Bible of the miraculous and retain only its moral principles. All this, of course, helped to fasten people's gaze on the here-and-now.

If a millenium was ever to come, man himself must bring it about, people decided. The second coming of Christ, that climactic miracle, seemed a virtual impossibility.

The empire of Christ seemed greatly constricted at the beginning of the nineteenth century. But then a unique movement began which shook the church to its foundations.

People began rediscovering a very important part of Scripture—the promise of Christ's second coming. They found that this wasn't just a hope confined to certain apocalyptic passages or to certain portions of the Bible, but a hope that animated all the writers of Scripture. There are over 2,500 references to the second coming. These men and women began studying unfulfilled prophecies in earnest. Societies were formed, journals published, conferences convened—all to promote the study of Scripture.

The Advent movement had begun. The champions of the second coming of Christ began to make their voices heard and turn people's hopes upward again.

The movement came to Paris through the writings of

Robert Gaussen, a French-Swiss Evangelical professor from Geneva. In the midst of a Geneva contented with a tamed, rationalistic religion, Gaussen rediscovered the amazingly accurate prophecy of Daniel 2, that sweeping portrayal of the succession of Babylon, Medo-Persia, Greece, and Rome. His faith in God's Word was strengthened and he took a stand, rejecting the theories of men for the gospel of Jesus Christ.

Gaussen became a zealous advocate of the consummation of that gospel: the second coming of the Saviour. He wrote eloquently about it and lifted the thoughts of those promenading down Paris's Champs Élysées to a coming kingdom.

The Advent awakening spread through Europe. In England, Edward Irving spoke to crowds of 10,000 or more at open air meetings about the imminence of the Advent. In Sweden, the state church forbade its ministers to engage in this unsettling talk about Christ coming in the clouds to swallow up all earthly dominions. So children spearheaded the movement. Crowds watched amazed as kids barely able to read gave moving expositions on prophecy. Their preaching lead to widespread revival in southern Sweden.

The Advent awakening spread to South America through the writings of a Spanish Jesuit named Lacunza. In a time of barbarism and superstition, this priest found his way to a study of Bible prophecy and became convicted that he must give a warning of the impending return of Christ.

Joseph Wolff, perhaps the ablest ambassador of the Advent Awakening, brought the message to India. Fluent in six languages, Wolff outlined the prophecies of Revelation to learned rabbis, Hindu holy men, Moslem imams, shahs, sheiks, kings, and queens.

Wolff even discovered Muslim tribes who still clung to a belief in the speedy arrival of the Messiah in the clouds of heaven. Everywhere he distributed Bibles and proclaimed that history would soon climax in the second coming of Christ.

In the United States, the Advent movement reached a climax with the powerful preaching of a former atheist, William Miller. His expositions of prophecy shook many churches throughout New England.

And out of this general awakening, the denomination I belong to was born as a reform movement: the Seventh-day Adventist Church.

In the midst of a world and church gazing on the earth, ambassadors of the coming kingdom fearlessly proclaimed that the empire of Christ was what really mattered. The future belonged to Christ alone.

This is the message that strikes at the heart of Satan's empire. And he seeks zealously to oppose it. Here is where the ultimate battle line will be drawn when the two empires clash in a final showdown. Who owns the future?

Which empire is eternal? Which will be destroyed?

One August day in 1944, Sergeant Milt Shenton learned that he was going to be the "point man," leading the Fourth Division of the U.S. Army into Paris. That meant he would become the first tempting target the German defenders of the city would sight.

Sergeant Shenton had had the same job on June 6, D-Day, when he led his division across Utah Beach. Amazingly, he'd survived unscathed. But Shenton figured that was all the luck any one man had a right to in a lifetime.

Muttering to himself, Shenton strapped an extra canister of ammunition to his jeep and headed down the empty, menacing street into Paris. Suddenly a window creaked open. The sergeant whirled around and pointed his carbine.

Then another window opened, and another. From somewhere he heard a woman's voice call out, "Les Americains!" Two women in bathrobes, their slippers flopping on the pavement, bolted for the jeep. Suddenly a man was beside Shenton, embracing him and kissing him on both cheeks.

Within seconds a horde of happy, shouting Parisians rushed out of the buildings and filled the street. The soldier who'd felt so alone and vulnerable a moment before was overwhelmed by a sea of exulting, tearful faces.

This was liberation, the day Paris had waited for through the long night of Nazi occupation. Finally they were free. No more German soldiers patrolling their streets. No more Gestapo beatings. No more Jews deported to death camps. No more resistance fighters lined up and shot. The years of frustration and fear and hunger had ended, this day, this moment.

Everywhere in the city it was the same, deliriously happy crowds rushed on the advancing American and French columns. Jeep drivers were crushed by the people eager to kiss them, touch them, talk to them. Hordes of children clung to tanks and armored cars like bunches of grapes. From sidewalks, people tossed flowers, carrots, radishes—anything they could offer.

They all wanted in some way to make this moment of liberation real. The years of occupation had seemed eternal; Hitler's power had seemed insurmountable at times. It was hard to believe that it was all over, that now they were really free again.

For many GI's these hours would be the most memorable of their lives. Little things stood out: an old French veteran with a handlebar mustache, a row of medals on his faded uniform, standing ramrod straight as the tanks rolled by, great tears rolling down his cheeks. A grandmother lying on a stretcher on the sidewalk, watching the liberators arrive through a mirror held over her head, repeating to the blue skies, "Paris is free, Paris is free."

There were unforgettable reunions that day. An American truck driver watched a woman run through a burst of gunfire and fall on an advancing French infantryman sobbing, "My son, my son."

A French corporal passed handwritten messages to the crowd from his tank, asking for his brother. He'd received no word from him in three years. In the heart of Paris the corporal suddenly noticed a figure making his way slowly down the line of tanks behind him. He stopped his tank and stared in disbelief. There, incredibly thin, in a policeman's uniform much too big for him, wearing a resistance armband, was his long-lost brother. The two men, who symbolized the two halves of fighting France, fell into each other's arms as if pushed by an electric current.

Together at last. Free at last.

Yes, the empire of Christ is going to burst into view some day soon as surely as those jeeps and tanks rolled into Paris. It's going to be a great day, the Liberation of Planet Earth. We've been in this long night of frustration and fear for so long. We've been so long under occupation by an enemy. Sometimes it's hard to believe liberation can be real.

But it's coming! The King is coming. And He's going to wipe away every tear. He's going to wipe out every fear. No more wars maiming and scarring another generation of the young. No more starving children with sad, bulging eyes and emaciated limbs. No more families torn apart. No more unending heartache for a lost loved one.

Oh, there will be exultation on that day! Delirious joy. Let me tell you, I'm longing for that day with all my heart. We'll be crowding around a glorified Jesus, longing to see and touch and talk to our Liberator. There will be shouting and singing and tears of joy. There will be wonderful reunions. We will be free at last.

This is the promise Christ's empire has been built on. This is the hope that has animated His people down through the ages—from the martyrs who shed their blood in the Colosseum, to the missionaries today giving their lives in every corner of the globe.

We must look up to the hope that Christ Himself offers. There is much to distract and seduce us. The religion of power beckons. The lawlessness of a world ignoring God's Word can overwhelm us. The promise of a material paradise whispers in our ears.

We must fix our hope altogether on Christ's kingdom, His empire. It is a hope that, if only we listen closely enough, can be heard echoing all over the world, in every part of Christ's marvelous empire of righteousness.

The Christ who was lifted up from our planet closes His Word with the wonderful promise, "Behold, I am coming soon." And then He extends an invitation, an invitation that all within Christ's kingdom repeat: "The Spirit and the bride say, 'Come!' . . . Whoever is thirsty, let him come; and whoever wishes, let him take the free gift of the water of life" (Revelation 22:12, 17).

Don't let anything prevent you from coming into the right kingdom. The two empires will soon collide in a climactic showdown that will shake the earth to its foundations. Make sure your grip on the gospel, on Christ's sacrificial love, on the Creator, on His Word, is firm. I urge you to start looking up now.